A Day in the Life Of

A Ladybug

Ruth Owen

Ruby Tuesday Books

Little Acorns

Published in 2025 by Ruby Tuesday Books Ltd.

Editor: Mark J. Sachner
Design: Tammy West
Production: John Lingham

Photo Credits:
Alamy: 16 (Jurgen Kottmann); Nature Picture Library: 7 (Stephen Dalton), 13 (Nature Production); Science Photo Library: 20–21 (Claude Nuridsany & Marie Perrenou); Shutterstock: Cover (Fariya Graphics), 4 (nieriss), 5 (Mickey Why), 6 (Cornel Constantin), 8 (JulieK2), 10 (irin-k), 11 (Sinan Guzel), 12 (Susanne Photography & Rina 991), 14 (Tabish Hassan Khan), 15 (Distracted By Bugs), 17 (Radzas2008), 18 (Szabadi Jeno Tibor), 19 (Neil Bromhall), 22 (Tom Deer, irin-k, mehmetkrc, & chinahbzyg), 23 (Smeerjewegproducties, aaltair, & Protasov AN), 24 (mehmetkrc); Superstock: 9 (Matt Cole).

Library of Congress Control Number: 2024941196

Print (Hardback) ISBN 978-1-78856-498-4
Print (Paperback) ISBN 978-1-78856-499-1
ePub ISBN 978-1-78856-500-4

Published in Minneapolis, MN
Printed in the United States

www.rubytuesdaybooks.com

CONTENTS

Hello, Little Ladybug!

It is morning in a sunny backyard.

A ladybug peeks from her
cozy hiding place in a bug hotel.

The little **beetle** is hungry.

It is time to go hunting!

The ladybug lifts up her red, spotted wing cases.

She unfolds her long, see-through wings.

Whoosh

Off she flies to look for food.

Ladybugs and other beetles are all **insects**.

The ladybug lands on a plant.

There are tiny insects called aphids on the plant's leaves.

Munch Munch Munch

Aphids are a ladybug's favorite food.

A ladybug eats about 50 aphids each day.

Sometimes the ladybug eats **pollen** from flowers.

When she needs a drink,
she sips water from raindrops.

A hungry bird sees
the ladybug.
Is she in danger?

No! The ladybug's red
color tells the bird that
she tastes bad.

Ladybugs make a stinky, yellow gloop that comes out of their legs.

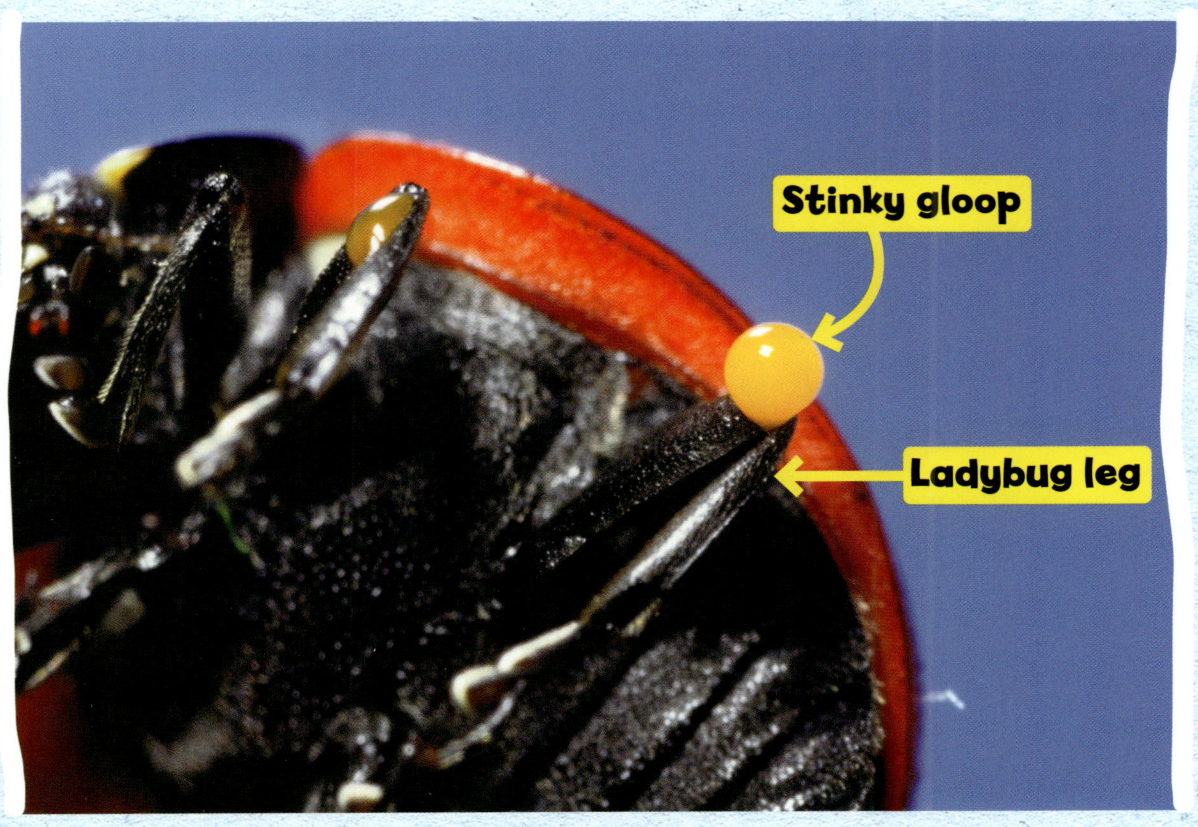

This keeps **predators** from eating them.

A few days ago, the ladybug **mated** with a male ladybug.

Today, she is ready to lay eggs. 

The ladybug lays her tiny yellow eggs under a leaf.

A ladybug can lay about 300 eggs.

After laying her eggs, the ladybug eats more aphids.

Munch

Munch

Munch

Then she finds a cozy hiding place to spend the night.

What will happen to the ladybug's eggs?

A baby ladybug called a **larva** hatches from each egg.

The larva eats aphids and gets bigger.

After three weeks, the larva becomes a **pupa**.

Now lots of changes happen.

After a few days, the pupa's case splits open.

A tiny yellow beetle climbs from the case.

After a few hours, the insect turns red and grows spots.

It's a new ladybug!

Glossary

beetle

A type of insect with wings and two hard wing cases or covers.

insect

A tiny animal with six legs. Ladybugs, butterflies, and bees are all insects.

larva

A young insect that hatches from an egg.

mate

To come together to produce young.

pollen
Dust made by flowers that helps plants make seeds and new plants.

predator
An animal that eats other animals.

pupa
A stage in the life cycle of some insects. Inside its pupa case, an insect changes into an adult.

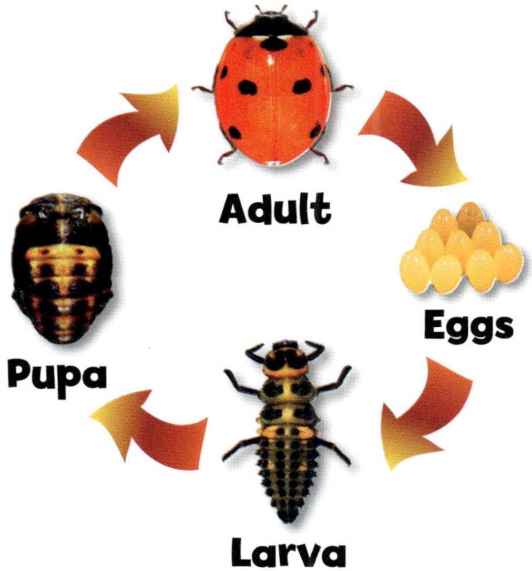

Index